NORTH AMERICA'S
BIGGEST BEASTS

BISON

David Anthony

PowerKiDS
press.

New York

Published in 2016 by The Rosen Publishing Group, Inc.
29 East 21st Street, New York, NY 10010

First Edition

Editor: Katie Kawa
Book Design: Reann Nye

Photo Credits: Cover (bison), pp. 1, 22 Eric Isselee/Shutterstock.com; cover (background) Don Fink/Shutterstock.com; p. 4 Pal Teravagimov/Shutterstock.com; p. 5 turtix/Shutterstock.com; p. 6 sergioboccardo/Shutterstock.com; p. 7 gibleho/Shutterstock.com; pp. 8–9 (background) Geoffrey Kuchera/Shutterstock.com; p. 9 (map) boreala/Shutterstock.com; p. 11 IrinaK/Shutterstock.com; p. 12 Jan Kratochvila/Shutterstock.com; p. 13 tab62/Shutterstock.com; p. 14 Elliot Hurwitt/Shutterstock.com; p. 15 Darren Baker/Shutterstock.com; p. 16 Derek R. Audette/Shutterstock.com; p. 17 Georgii Shipin/Shutterstock.com; p. 18 https://commons.wikimedia.org/wiki/File:Kane_Assiniboine_hunting_buffalo.jpg; p. 19 Ronnie Howard/Shutterstock.com; p. 21 visceralimage/Shutterstock.com.

Library of Congress Cataloging-in-Publication Data

Anthony, David, 1971- author.
 Bison / David Anthony.
    pages cm. — (North America's biggest beasts)
 Includes index.
 ISBN 978-1-5081-4288-1 (pbk.)
 ISBN 978-1-5081-4284-3 (6 pack)
 ISBN 978-1-5081-4289-8 (library binding)
 1. American bison—Juvenile literature. I. Title.
 QL737.U53A548 2016
 599.64'3—dc23
                                    2015022271

Manufactured in the United States of America

CPSIA Compliance Information: Batch #BW16PK: For Further Information contact Rosen Publishing, New York, New York at 1-800-237-9932

CONTENTS

Massive Land Mammals

Many large **mammals** walk the lands of North America, but none are heavier than the bison. Bison are the largest land mammals in North America. They can weigh more than 1 ton. That's the same as 2,000 pounds (907 kg)!

There are two main species, or kinds, of bison. The European bison lives in Europe, and the American bison is found in North America. Millions of American bison used to live in the part of North America known as the Great Plains.

African buffalo

THE BIG IDEA

American bison are sometimes called "buffaloes," but that name is incorrect. Buffaloes are animals that look somewhat like bison, but they live in Africa and Asia.

It's believed that over 50 million bison once lived on the Great Plains. However, by 1889, there were fewer than 1,000 bison alive in the wild in North America because of overhunting and **damage** to their **habitat**.

Bison Body Basics

Bison are heavy mammals, and they're also tall. An adult male bison can stand as tall as 6.5 feet (2 m) at the shoulder. Females are smaller than males. Both males and females have curved horns that end in a sharp tip.

A bison's fur is dark brown. The fur is longest on the bison's head, neck, and shoulders. A bison also has a very large head and a hump at its shoulders. It uses its head and hump to push away snow in the winter in order to find food.

For being a very heavy mammal, a bison can move surprisingly quickly! That's just one thing about bison that makes them such special animals.

WHAT'S SO SPECIAL ABOUT BISON?

SENSES
Bison have strong senses of smell and hearing.

SPEED
Bison can run at speeds of up to 40 miles (64.4 km) per hour.

HEAD & HUMP
Bison use their head and hump to dig for food under the snow.

JUMPING
Bison can jump up to 6 feet (1.8 m) in the air.

SIZE
Bison are the largest land mammals in North America.

FUR
Fur keeps bison warm during harsh winters on the Great Plains.

A Bison's Habitat

A bison's size and strength were very important for its **survival** on the Great Plains. This habitat is the area of grassland that runs from the Mississippi River westward to the Rocky Mountains. The winters can be very cold on the Great Plains, while the summers can be very hot.

Bison once lived in large numbers on the Great Plains. Now, they live in much smaller numbers on **protected** areas of open land throughout North America. They also live on ranches and in zoos.

THE BIG IDEA

While most bison called the Great Plains home, a much smaller number lived in northwestern Canada and Alaska. This kind of bison is called the wood bison. Wood bison can be seen today on protected lands in Canada.

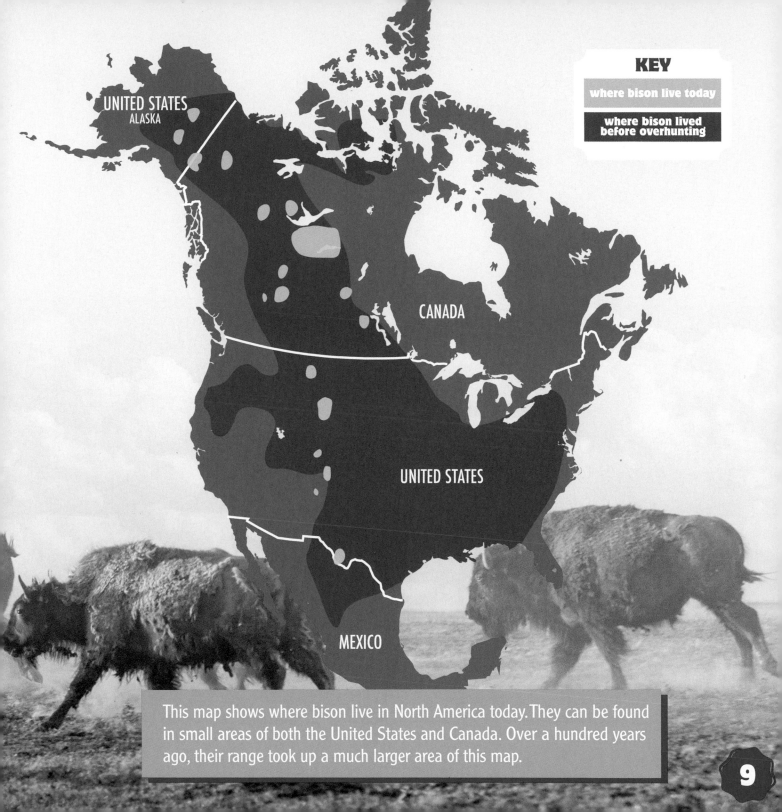

UNITED STATES
ALASKA

CANADA

UNITED STATES

MEXICO

This map shows where bison live in North America today. They can be found in small areas of both the United States and Canada. Over a hundred years ago, their range took up a much larger area of this map.

Great Grazers

The Great Plains is a perfect habitat for bison because it's an area of grassland, and grasses are bison's favorite foods. Many **herbs** also grow on the Great Plains, and bison like to eat herbs, too. If food is hard to come by, which often happens in the winter, bison will eat twigs.

Bison graze, or eat grasses, throughout the day. When millions of bison lived in the wild, large groups would travel south in the winter and north when the weather got warmer again in order to find more food.

Because bison are such large animals, they need to eat a lot of grass. They eat about 2 **percent** of their body weight in grass each day.

Ready for the Rut

Male bison are called bulls, and female bison are called cows. During the summer, adult bulls and cows mate, or come together to make babies. The mating season for bison is also called the rut. During this time, a bull follows his chosen cow around and fights other bulls that try to get too close.

Bison often wallow, or roll around in mud, more than usual during the rut. When bison wallow, they leave behind large **depressions** in the ground because of their large body.

ACTION	WHAT'S IT CALLED?	WHAT DOES IT LEAVE BEHIND?
rolling around in the mud or shallow water	wallowing	wallow: large depression in the ground with no plants in it
walking over a wide area of land	roaming	hoof prints: circular marks from bison's hoofs on the ground
rubbing horns against a tree	tree horning	worn areas on trees from bison's horns

Bison leave signs that they were in an area, especially during the rut.

Baby Bison

After the rut, it takes around 9 months before a cow has a baby bison, or calf. A cow only gives birth to one calf at a time. At birth, calves generally weigh between 30 and 40 pounds (13.6 and 18.1 kg), and they have reddish fur when they're born. Calves drink milk from their mother until they're around one year old.

During this first year, cows take care of their young. Bulls don't care for calves. Young bison often stay with their mother's herd. Each herd has its own social order.

THE BIG IDEA

Calves can stand and walk on their own minutes after they're born.

Calves are much smaller than adult bison, but they're still larger than many other adult mammals!

Bison in Danger

Cows protect their calves from other animals that hunt them. Calves and bison that are old or sick are in the most danger of being killed by predators. These predators include mountain lions and wolves.

Healthy adult bison are big, strong, and fast enough to avoid becoming another animal's meal. However, there was one predator who was too powerful for bison to escape, and that was people. Guns used by hunters made it possible for people to kill very large numbers of bison in a short period of time.

wolf pack

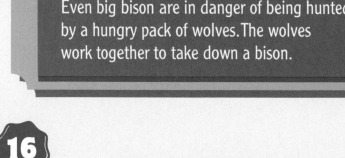

Even big bison are in danger of being hunted by a hungry pack of wolves. The wolves work together to take down a bison.

A Respected Animal

Before Europeans came to North America, the only people who hunted bison were the Native Americans who lived on the Great Plains. These Native Americans believed in using every part of the bison after they killed it. This massive mammal gave the Native Americans meat to eat, hides and fur for clothing and shelter, and bones for tools.

Because the Native Americans used every part of the bison and treated the animal with respect, they didn't often hunt bison in very large numbers.

The Native Americans who lived on the Great Plains respected bison enough not to overhunt them. Other people who lived on the Great Plains after them didn't share the same respect for bison.

THE BIG IDEA

A white bison is a bison with white fur. This animal was especially honored by Native Americans.

Almost a Lost Species

As Americans moved westward in the 1800s, they began killing more bison. Some they hunted for food, and others they hunted for sport. To kill such a huge animal was seen as a big accomplishment among hunters during this time.

Bison were also killed because of their importance to Native Americans. Taking away bison made it easier to force Native Americans off lands new settlers wanted. By the time the 1900s began, bison were almost **extinct** in North America because of overhunting.

THE BIG IDEA

The construction of railroads across the Great Plains took important grasslands away from bison. Without grasses to eat, even more bison died.

Bison are mighty mammals, but they almost didn't survive as a species because of the actions of people.

Saving the Bison

In the early 1900s, people in both the United States and Canada joined together to find a way to protect the bison that were left. The remaining bison were moved to protected lands, zoos, and ranches. Now there are around 500,000 bison living in North America.

Bison are still the largest land mammals in North America by size, even if they're not as big in numbers as they once were. You can often see these huge animals up close in zoos or even some national parks!

Glossary

damage: Loss or harm done to a person or piece of property.

depression: A flattened area of land where the center is lower than the land around it.

extinct: No longer existing.

habitat: The natural home for plants, animals, and other living things.

herb: A low-growing plant used to make medicine or give food flavor.

mammal: Any warm-blooded animal whose babies drink milk and whose body is covered with hair or fur.

percent: A part of a whole, measured in parts of a hundred.

protected: Kept safe.

survival: The state of continuing to live.

Index

Websites

Due to the changing nature of Internet links, PowerKids Press has developed an
online list of websites related to the subject of this book. This site is updated regularly.
Please use this link to access the list: www.powerkidslinks.com/nabb/bison